HUMAN BODY

EXTREME FACTS

BY STEFFI CAVELL-CLARKE

©2017
The Secret Book Company
King's Lynn
Norfolk PE30 4LS

ISBN: 978-1-912171-19-4

Written by:
Steffi Cavell-Clarke
Edited by:
Holly Duhig
Designed by:
Danielle Rippengill

A catalogue record for this book is available from the British Library

THE SECRET BOOK COMPANY

PHOTO CREDITS

Abbreviations: l-left, r-right, b-bottom, t-top, c-centre, m-middle.

2-3 – toeytoey. 4t – Art Painter, 4b – Choksawatdikorn. 5 – Doors. 7 tl – Oxana Gracheva, 7mr – Shaijo, 7b – Deviney Designs. 9tl – Rattiya Thongdumhyu, 9tr – Background All, 9m – Choksawatdikorn. 11tl – Ed Clark, 11bl – UGREEN 3S, 11br – Choksawatdikorn. 12 – toeytoey. 13tl – noidec, 13tr – Ravennka, 13b – Art Painter. 15tl – Adrian_am13, 15r – Bogachyova Arina, 15bl – s.juchim. 16t – Imageman, 16b – Freedom_Studio. 17t – Mr.prasong, 17m – Arts Vector. 18 – AkeSak. 19tr – Arts Vector, 19mr – Bildagentur Zoonar GmbH, 19bl – toeytoey. 20m – VolenV., 20br – SingjaiStock. 21t – ANUCHA PONGPATIMETH, 21mr – Mr.prasong. 22 – Dmitry A. 23tl – sripfoto, 23br – Background All.

Images are courtesy of Shutterstock.com. With thanks to Getty Images, Thinkstock Photo and iStockphoto.

CONTENTS

Words that look like <u>this</u> can be found in the glossary on page 24.

THE HUMAN BODY

Have you ever wondered what lies under your skin? Have you ever thought about what happens when someone breaks a bone? There is a lot to discover about the human body, so let's begin!

We all look different on the outside, but we are all the same on the inside. Our bodies all need need **air**, **water** and **sleep** to survive.

Our bodies are all made up of bones, muscles, organs, blood and skin.

Nose

Eye

Head

Chest

Mouth

Hand

Arm

Leg

Fingers

Toes

Foot

BONES

Everybody has a skeleton that is made up of many bones.

Bones give your body structure, they let you move around and they protect your <u>internal</u> organs.

You have 206 bones in your body.

Over half of the bones in your body are in your hands and feet.

An adult's skull is made up of 22 bones.

X 22 =

Your bones are alive! They grow and change all the time, just like the rest of your body.

Your thighbone is the largest and strongest bone in your body.

The smallest bones in your body are found in your ears.

If a bone breaks, it can repair itself.

X-rays let doctors see what's going on inside a person's body.

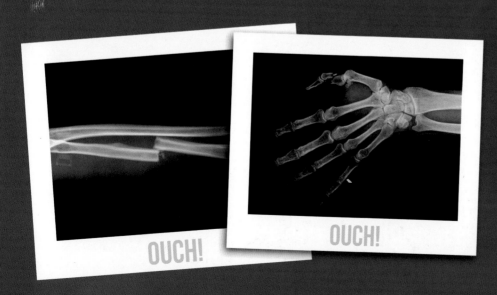

OUCH!

OUCH!

X-rays can be used to look at your bones to see if you have broken any.

MUSCLES

Muscles do a lot of things!

The heart is a muscle that helps pump blood through your body.

Other muscles help you move and lift things.

There are over

640

muscles in the human body.

You use

200

muscles just to take one step.

Your tongue is one of the strongest muscles in your body.

Exercise can make your muscles bigger and stronger

Playing, running, jumping and swimming are just a few ways to make your muscles stronger.

The more you use your muscles, the stronger they will get.

Eating healthy food that contains lots of protein can help to make muscles stronger.

Protein is found in meat and fish.

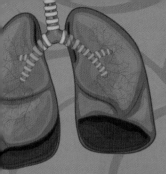

ORGANS

Each organ has a special job to do in the body.

Your lungs allow you to breathe air.

Your brain controls your body, the way you think and the way you react to the world around you.

?

The heart pumps blood all around the body. It is about the size of a fist.

Brain

Heart

Lungs

Liver

Stomach

Kidneys

Spleen

Large Intestine

Small Intestine

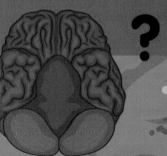

Your kidneys look like giant kidney beans. They filter about 189 litres of blood every day.

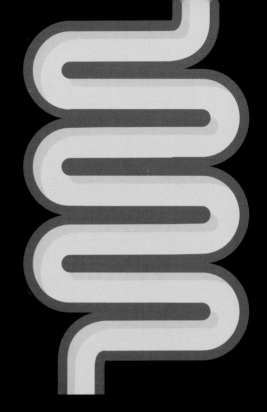

The liver cleans your blood.

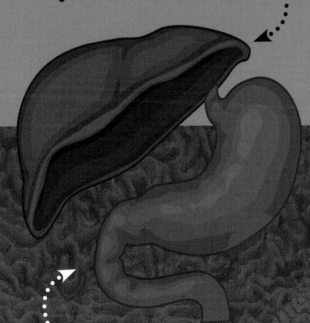

Your intestines are part of your digestive system. Your small intestine is about 6 metres long!

Your stomach breaks down the food you eat.

Your spleen is soft, purple and filters your blood. However, it is possible to live without it!

BLOOD

Blood is a red <u>liquid</u> that is found throughout your entire body.

The average person has 4-6 litres of blood in their body.

Your blood helps you to fight <u>infections</u>.

The blood's job is to carry <u>oxygen</u> around the body and remove <u>carbon dioxide</u>.

It also carries heat around the body to help keep your body warm. Clever blood!

Our blood is made up of lots of tiny units called cells.

If you lose a lot of blood in one go, you can die.

The cells that make up your blood float in a yellow liquid called plasma.

Some people <u>donate</u> their blood to help others who have lost a lot of blood.

SKIN

Skin covers the body and is the largest organ.

It protects your bones, muscles and organs from infection.

If your skin gets damaged, it can repair itself.

Most people's skin sweats out about 1,000 litres of liquid per year.

Most of your skin is covered in a soft layer of hair.

The hair on your head grows at an average rate of around 15 centimetres per year.

Your nails and hair are dead. That's why it doesn't hurt when you have them cut.

The longest hair ever recorded was **5.6 metres long!**

SENSES

Human beings have five main senses.

Taste (tongue)

You have up to 10,000 taste buds on your tongue.

The record for the longest tongue is 10.1 centimetres.

Sight (eyes)

You blink about 6,205,000 times a year.

Touch (skin)

Your fingertips, lips and feet are some of the most sensitive parts of your body.

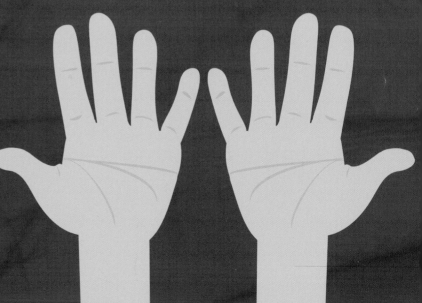

Smell (nose)

Our noses also keep us healthy by stopping germs from entering our lungs.

Noses have special cells in them that help you to smell.

Did you know that your nose and ears will never stop growing?

Hearing (ears)

You have tiny hairs deep inside your ears. If you lose these hairs, then you will lose your hearing.

BREATHING

When you breathe, you are using your respiratory system.

Your respiratory system is the group of organs in your body that allow you to breathe.

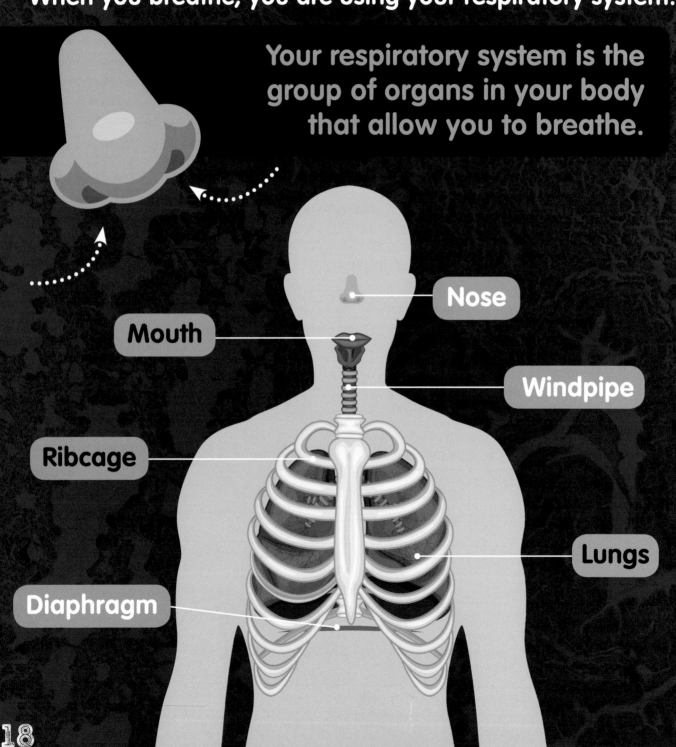

Nose

Mouth

Windpipe

Ribcage

Lungs

Diaphragm

The respiratory system takes **oxygen** into the body and gets rid of carbon dioxide.

Your respiratory system can also make you cough, sneeze and get the hiccups.

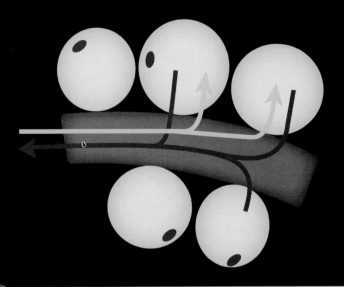

You use both your lungs to breathe, but people can survive with just one working lung.

Without oxygen, the cells in your body will die.

The average human takes about 7 million breaths in one year.

MOVING

It is important that we move our bodies and exercise.

Exercise makes you stronger and healthier.

Playing football, riding a bike and walking to school are all good forms of exercise.

Exercising will help to keep your weight at a healthy level and reduce your risk of getting ill.

Exercise can help to make you feel happy.

It is also important that we rest our bodies.

When you are sleeping, your body is repairing itself.

If you have hurt yourself, then you will need to rest to give your body time to heal.

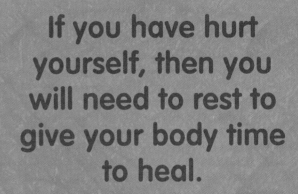

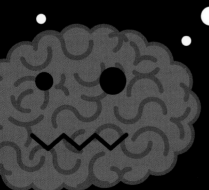

Your brain cannot work properly without a good night's sleep.

EATING

Your digestive system is what allows you to get <u>energy</u> from the food you eat.

Your digestive system breaks food down into small pieces.

It takes <u>nutrients</u> from the food and uses them to keep your body healthy.

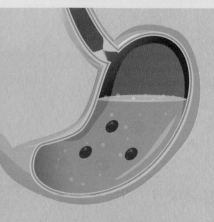

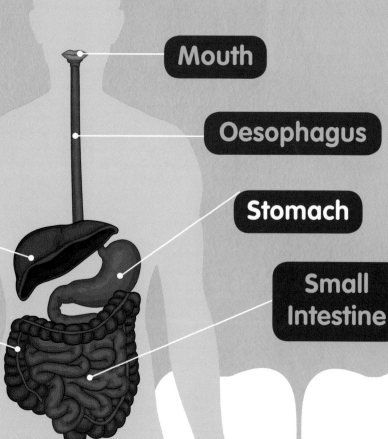

Mouth

Oesophagus

Liver

Stomach

Large Intestine

Small Intestine

Some foods give our bodies energy. They are called carbohydrates.

FLOUR

Fruit **and vegetables** help our bodies to stay healthy.

Don't forget that it's important to eat a healthy, balanced diet.

It is also important to drink water to stay <u>hydrated</u>.

23

GLOSSARY

carbon dioxide	a natural, colourless gas that is found in the air
digestive system	the bodily system that digests food
donate	to give something away for a good cause, such as charity
energy	the strength needed for physical and mental activity
hydrated	to have enough water
infections	illnesses caused by dirt, germs and bacteria getting into the body
internal	located inside something, such as the body
liquid	a material that flows, such as water
nutrients	natural substances that people need to grow and stay healthy
oxygen	a natural gas that all living things need in order to survive

INDEX